NEW YORK CITY

Produced by
ALBION PUBLISHING GROUP
924 Anacapa Street, Suite 3A
Santa Barbara, CA 93101

Managing Editor
MARIE L. HATHAWAY

Art Director
JOANNE STATION

Editor
ANNE Du BOIS

Contributing Editors
JIM ANDERSON, JOAN OLIVER,
CHRISTINA SIMON

Editorial Contributors
BRADFORD HILL, SUSANNA PASHKO

Writers
L. J. DUMOND, ANN MERLIN

PHOTO GRAPHICS

©1992 Impact

Printed in Hong Kong
ISBN 1-56540-033-X

▲
Set just inside Central Park at 67th Street, and decorated in a free-form style, Tavern on the Green does more business than any other restaurant in New York. The spectacle of the thousands of tiny fairy lights on the restaurant's facade and strung on the trees outside is unrivaled, even in New York City.

Bethesda Fountain at the edge of the lake in Central Park is a popular meeting place for New Yorkers. This was a favorite of nineteenth-century residents, as well. During the summer months, such street performers as Dixieland bands, magicians, and stilt walkers enliven the area that stretches from the fountain down the mall. ▶

FRONT COVER: Reminiscent, perhaps, of the Manhattan of the imagination, a purple-hued dusk silhouettes Lower Manhattan, South Street Seaport, and the Brooklyn Bridge. The city seems to beckon visitors to explore and enjoy what it has to offer.

INSIDE FRONT COVER & PAGE 1: There are sections of New York that look as though they are from another time, another place. The old Greenwich Village homes pictured here are a charming and refreshing change from the massive Manhattan apartment structures where most New Yorkers live.

PAGES 2 & 3: These fanciful murals on the side of an ordinary apartment building in SoHo show that not all the art worth seeing in New York is in the galleries and museums. Such whimsical works placed in the environment provide a moment of lightness to all who pass by.

CONTENTS

PART 1

LOWER MANHATTAN

PAGE 6: The nation celebrated the Statue of Liberty's one-hundredth anniversary in 1986. Named *Liberty Enlightening the World* by her sculptor, Frederic August Bartholdi, the statue is sometimes referred to as the Lady in the Harbor. A gift to the people of the United States from the people of France—and paid for by French schoolchildren—the majestic Lady is a symbol of freedom to people all over the world.

PAGE 7: A Lower East Side bakery offers *knishes* (the *k* and the *n* are pronounced). This Yiddish pastry, which originated in Russia, is made of a thin crust wrapped around different fillings. The most traditional are potato, but there are also cheese, cherry-cheese, spinach, and *kasha* (buckwheat-groat) knishes.

The historic lower Manhattan district of the South Street Seaport is being restored to resemble its former glory as one of the world's great ports for sailing vessels. You'll want to visit the vintage ships, museum, old-fashioned print shop, seafood restaurants, the popular Fulton Fish Market, the Titanic Memorial Lighthouse, and the many modern shops.

New York City! People in neighboring states call it the City, and around the country it's known as the Big Apple. The 7.3 million people who live, work, and play in the abundance that New York has to offer call it home, whether they're movie stars, cab drivers, diplomats, grocers, bankers, or students.

But when Giovanni da Verrazano, the first European explorer to venture into New York Bay, saw this region from the deck of his ship in April 1524, it appeared to be nothing but an impenetrable wilderness. Verrazano never actually landed; instead, he sailed around the lower bay—just downstream from where the bridge now bearing his name would be erected some four hundred years later.

It wasn't until 1609 that another European, Henry Hudson, actually set foot on the land that would one day become the busy core of New York City, the island-borough known as Manhattan. In later years the Dutch West India Company set up shop here, calling it Nieuw (New) Amsterdam; but the British claimed it for themselves in 1664, naming it New York, for their king's brother, the Duke of York.

New York City was conceived in lower Manhattan. This is where the Dutch purchased the island from the Algonquian Indians in 1626 for that legendary twenty-four dollars' worth of trinkets—a shrewd financial bargain, and a fitting beginning for what is now one of the world's busiest financial districts. Three centuries later, *Wall Street* is a well-known metaphor for New York's prestige as an international center of finance.

Farther up Manhattan—between Houston (pronounced *How-ston*) Street at the north and the Brooklyn Bridge at the south—pockets of ethnic diversity thrive in the communities of Chinatown, Little Italy, and the Lower East Side. These neighborhoods, where people still speak the languages of their immigrant ancestors, are reminders of the origins of all Americans.

West of the Bowery and the Lower East Side, and south of Houston Street, are the areas of SoHo and Tribeca. SoHo, which stands for <u>south of Houston</u>, is best known for the highest concentration of artists and galleries in New York (see Art in N. Y. C. on pages 16 and 17). Tribeca, an acronym for <u>triangle below Canal</u>, has gained a reputation as a growing artists' community and for its gourmet food shops, nightclubs, and restaurants.

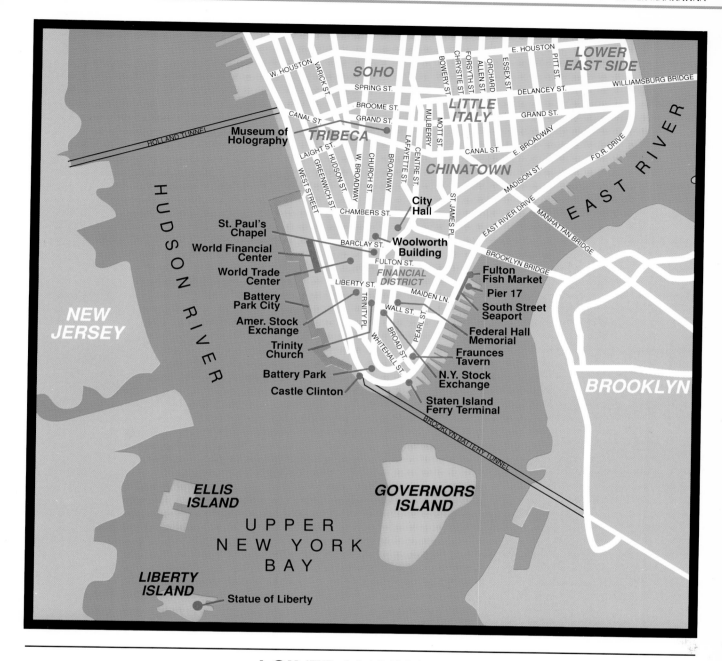

LOWER MANHATTAN

Map not to scale. For a more complete listing of helpful area maps, please turn to page 64.

► The fresh, raw ingredients for Chinese cuisine can be found in the open markets on eastern Canal Street: fish, meat, exotic vegetables, and fruits are sold in shops and stalls along its south side between Centre and Mulberry streets.

◄ At 110-stories tall, and visible from just about everywhere in New York City, the World Trade Center's twin towers seem almost too big to be real. In the south tower, take one of the fastest elevators you'll ever ride in—1,377 feet up to the open-air observation deck; you'll have a 360-degree view of the greater New York area. A stop here on a clear day should be mandatory for every visitor to New York.

◄ Chinatown is more insulated from the influence of New York than are most of the other ethnic neighborhoods in lower Manhattan. Chinese heritage is highly visible here in customs, food, and language, and as you stroll the streets you might momentarily think you're in old Canton.

At the southern tip of Manhattan is historic Battery Park, named for the battery of cannons that were once lined up to protect the island. Before the immigration facilities at Ellis Island were constructed, immigrants disembarked from their ships at this site. Between 1855 and 1891 these new Americans were processed here through what is now called Castle Clinton National Monument. ►

▲

Some twenty million immigrants passed through Ellis Island between 1891 and 1954, the year the island was closed. These travelers, who endured many weeks of difficult ocean voyage, knew this place as the Isle of Tears, for they were afraid of not passing the immigration requirements and being returned to their homelands. The Immigration Museum, located in the main building, displays documents, photographs, and personal possessions that provide poignant insight into the story of immigration.

◄ This early 1900s view of Hester Street shows a typical street scene of that era. Many immigrants typically did their shopping for the day in open-air markets like this. Peddlers paid only twenty-five dollars a year for a license to do business. Soft pretzels, hot dogs, *knishes* (Yiddish pastries), and nonedible merchandise are still sold on the sidewalks of New York today.

THE IMMIGRANTS

It is the flag just as much of the [person] who was naturalized yesterday as of the [person] whose people have been here many generations.

—HENRY CABOT LODGE

If New York City could be defined by any one thing, it would be the number and diversity of its neighborhoods, which are themselves defined by the mosaic of their ethnic and cultural heritages. By their very arrival, immigrants changed the character of cities all over the United States—and especially that of New York. Areas with nicknames like Little Italy and Chinatown bear witness to this: on streets such as Mulberry, Mott, and Hester on the Lower East Side, and in the ethnic neighborhoods of Brooklyn, the Bronx, and Queens, is found a multicultural stew of nationalities.

The greatest waves of immigration took place from the 1840s through the 1920s. Uprooting themselves from relatives and homelands, immigrants came to America for two main reasons: personal freedom and economic opportunity. Many settled on the Lower East Side among friends or family or to be near those who spoke a familiar language and who shared the same culture and religion. The district was also close to the industrial areas that provided income for the skilled and unskilled immigrant laborer.

These neighborhoods were not the oppressive ghettos of their European counterparts. The American ghetto provided hospitality, jobs, political contacts, and economic opportunities for the new immigrant. Neighborhood schools and settlement houses also served to integrate people of various cultures into the larger community.

These new Americans witnessed changes in their traditional lifestyles that had included a clearly defined family structure. The father could not always find work that would allow him to provide adequately for his family. And the mother, who could once have depended on a network of extended family and friends, often found herself isolated. The immigrant parents expected their children to become better educated and more successful.

For these youngsters, the schoolroom offered both a cultural transition and a first step toward becoming part of the wider society of New York. Often they were the only bridge for their parents between Old World traditions and New World expectations. The children could speak, read, and write English, and their earning power usually surpassed their parents'. Thus the dream of the immigrants—that life would be better in America than in their homelands—saw the beginning of its fulfillment in their children.

Some first- and second-generation immigrant children who grew up to make names for themselves in America include industrialist and philanthropist Andrew Carnegie, composer Irving Berlin, scientist and author Isaac Asimov, children's author Maya Wojciechowska, and writers J. D. Salinger (*Catcher in the Rye*), Frances Eliza Hodgson Burnett (*The Secret Garden*), and William Saroyan (*The Human Comedy*).

A newly arrived Italian family aboard an Immigration Service ferry is being transferred from their ship's landing pier to Ellis Island in the early 1900s. The number of immigrants was so great during the peak immigration years that newcomers sometimes had to wait several days before making the short crossing to Ellis Island.

▲

The Manhattan Bridge, shown in the foreground, connects the boroughs of Manhattan and Brooklyn. Completed in 1909, it was one of the first suspension bridges to use just two cables. Unlike the Brooklyn Bridge, shown in the background, the more-modern Manhattan Bridge incorporated the use of structural steel in its towers, juxtaposing modern engineering with the ornateness of nineteenth-century architecture.

Housed behind the handsome Greek Revival facade on Wall Street is the New York Stock Exchange. Nicknamed the Big Board, it is the center of the financial district. You may be amazed at the frantic trading that you can see from the public gallery on the second floor. Knowledgeable tour guides will help you unravel the mysteries of this important securities market.

 City Hall is both a historic and functioning civic capital. One of the most-beautiful public buildings in the country, it was built between 1803 and 1811 and underwent extensive renovation in 1956. The historical Governor's Room on the second floor is open to the public. Elegantly furnished in the Federal style, it contains priceless portraits of America's early leaders.

There actually was once a wall on what is now known as Wall Street: the early Dutch settlers built it for defense against Indian attacks. In this turn-of-the-century photograph the building on the left is the Federal Hall National Memorial, at the corner of Wall and Nassau streets. George Washington took the presidential oath of office in this building on April 30, 1789.

ART IN N.Y.C.

Mention the words *art* and *New York City* in the same sentence, and many images come to mind: an Egyptian pharaoh's tomb in the Metropolitan Museum of Art, an exhibit of Pennsylvania Dutch–country quilts at the Museum of American Folk Art, or even an avant-garde exhibition in a SoHo artist's bathroom—New York City has it all.

The generosity of New York's philanthropists and its government has endowed the city with museums whose collections rival those anywhere in the world. Exhibitions at galleries and museums change constantly, and gallery hopping is a wonderful way to discover new artists, revel in the brilliance of the old masters, or simply enjoy some quiet moments.

The major galleries are concentrated in SoHo, midtown on 57th Street, and uptown on Madison Avenue. To plan an excursion, consult an *Art Now Gallery Guide*, available at galleries throughout the city. Museums of all types are located in New York City, and some have branch locations.

▲

The Guggenheim Museum was founded in 1939 to house modern art. It is the only building in New York designed by America's best-known architect, Frank Lloyd Wright. Start your tour at the top and walk down the spiraling ramp; you will be able to see every exhibit from anywhere in this circular building.

ART MUSEUMS

- American Craft Museum
- Museum of American Folk Art
- Center for African Art
- The Brooklyn Museum
- The Cloisters (branch of the Metropolitan Museum of Art)
- Museum of Contemporary Hispanic Art
- The Cooper-Hewitt Museum
- Dia Center for the Arts
- The Frick Collection
- The Solomon R. Guggenheim Museum
- International Center of Photography
- Metropolitan Museum of Art
- Municipal Art Society
- Museum of Modern Art (MOMA)
- National Academy of Design
- New Museum of Contemporary Art
- The Studio Museum in Harlem
- Whitney Museum of American Art

OTHER MUSEUMS

- American Museum of Natural History
- Asia Society (cultural & art)
- Museum of the American Indian (cultural)
- El Museo del Barrio (cultural)
- Brooklyn Children's Museum (natural history)
- Children's Museum of Manhattan (mixed)
- Museum of the City of New York (historical)
- Ellis Island Immigration Museum (cultural)
- Forbes Magazine Galleries (cultural; includes Fabergé eggs)
- Hayden Planetarium
- Museum of Holography
- The Jewish Museum at the New-York Historical Society (Jewish art; cultural)
- Museum of the Moving Image (cinema)
- Museum of TV & Broadcasting

One of the best ways to see the new trends in art, or simply to people watch, is to attend a gallery opening. SoHo has a high concentration of New York City galleries, and experimental artists generally show their work here. Uptown galleries are more chic and expensive, but there are hundreds throughout New York—enough to satisfy everyone's taste. ▶

◀ New York City has long been a mecca for foreign-born and American artists, as well as a subject for their artistic expression. The city's boundless energy can be seen in paintings from the Ash Can School of the early twentieth century to the paintings and sculptures of Abstract Expressionism of the 1940s and 1950s. This 1991 Postmodern creation by David Salle entitled *Honor Partners II* does justice to New York's tradition of modern art.

LET US RAISE A STANDARD TO WHICH
AND THE HONEST CAN REPAIR
IS IN THE HAND OF GOD

PART 2

GREENWICH VILLAGE, EAST VILLAGE & LOWER MANHATTAN NEIGHBORHOODS

PAGE 18: Washington Square Arch is at the northern end of Washington Square Park, and Fifth Avenue begins here. This is where many of Greenwich Village's residents spend their free time, as do the students of New York University, which surrounds much of the area. An unusual party winds through here on Hallowe'en, as costumed villagers uninhibitedly celebrate the holiday.

PAGE 19: Available from sidewalk vendors, the warm and salty soft pretzel seems to be a staple for New Yorkers. Also sold on the street is an impressive array of other tasty snack foods, including frankfurters, Greek souvlaki, Yiddish knishes, and hot chestnuts in winter.

Still one of Greenwich Village's evening social spots, the White Horse Tavern was Welsh poet Dylan Thomas's favorite bar when he lived in the Village in the early 1950s.

Greenwich Village—sometimes known as the West Village, or simply the Village—was originally a small, suburban hamlet to which city dwellers once escaped the summer's heat and humidity. The East Village was more rural: it was part of the farm, or *bouwerie,* once owned by Nieuw Amsterdam's governor, Peter Stuyvesant.

At the heart of Greenwich Village sits Washington Square. Its graceful marble arch was designed in the 1890s by architect Stanford White, a native New Yorker. The arch and the pink brick row houses at its northern edge are reminders of refined periods of the last century. Today the square bustles with activity, and nearby antique stores, book shops, boutiques, restaurants, and galleries charm visitor and resident alike. There are several small playhouses in the Village, which is also home to the New York Public Theater.

Greenwich Village's bohemian tradition began in the early 1900s. As the more-prosperous residents began moving uptown, artists, writers, and other nonconformists were attracted by its low rents and the presence of others of like mind. Eugene O'Neill, Edna St. Vincent Millay, Edward Hopper, and e. e. cummings are among those who lived here then. Former New York City mayor Ed Koch has made his home here, as have many famous people involved in the arts.

The Village has magical corners of serenity—tree-lined streets and graceful homes. Laid out according to original colonial pathways, the streets meander pleasantly through the neighborhood.

But many neighborhoods are changing in character. Past Broadway is the East Village, once a base for hippies in the 1960s and 1970s. It is now composed of moderately priced apartment buildings, shops, and businesses, as well as a growing art community.

At the intersection of Broadway and Fifth Avenue since 1902 is the wedge-shaped Flatiron Building. Its unique form has given both the building and the district their names. The newly renovated area now houses photography, publishing, and advertising businesses. Also here is an area known as the Photo District. Everything imaginable in photographic supplies is available for both amateur and professional photographers.

Chelsea lies to the northwest of Greenwich Village. Although it is mainly residential, there are several sites worth stopping for: at 222 West 23rd Street, the Chelsea Hotel's quaint red brick and lacy ironwork facade has discreetly accommodated such artists as Andy Warhol, Larry Rivers, and Julian Schnabel, as well as many writers and musicians, since its conversion from a town house in 1905. There are also well-tended brownstones, painted lively colors, on West 20th, 21st, and 22nd streets to wander among.

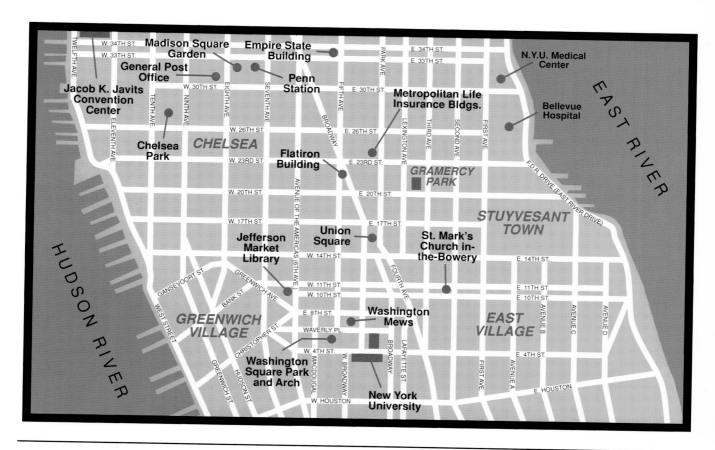

GREENWICH VILLAGE, EAST VILLAGE & LOWER MANHATTAN NEIGHBORHOODS

Map not to scale. For a more complete listing of helpful area maps, please turn to page 64.

The Jefferson Market Library, located at Greenwich Avenue and Ninth Street, is evidence of a community's effort to save a historic structure. The building, which was once a courthouse, was scheduled for demolition in 1945. It now houses a branch of the New York Public Library. The tower was added in 1877 as a fire lookout.

Since 1985 the glittering Jacob K. Javits Convention Center has attracted major conventions to its West 34th Street and Eleventh Avenue site near the Hudson. Fresh produce, fish, and Italian and Chinese delicacies are available at street markets on Ninth Avenue between West 39th and 40th streets. And a new theater section has evolved on West 42nd Street between Ninth and Tenth avenues.

Farther north is Clinton, an area that is often called Hell's Kitchen. This is a mixed-use district, where industrial buildings and apartment houses rub shoulders with restaurants and off–off-Broadway playhouses.

▲

When the Flatiron Building was built in 1902 at the intersection of Broadway and Fifth Avenue at 23rd Street, it was the tallest building in New York. Its unique triangular form gave the building its name. The term *23 skiddoo* was said to have originated from the fact that wind currents created by the Flatiron's shape had a tendency to lift the skirts of women shoppers along 23rd Street.

The Village Cigar Shop stands at the intersection of Christopher Street and Seventh Avenue, in the center of Greenwich Village. Christopher Street has a modern tradition of gay pride that can be traced to an evening in June 1969, when the gay patrons of a neighborhood bar stood up for their rights against harassment. ▶

▲
The monumental and glittering Jacob K. Javits Convention Center is located at the end of West 34th Street near the Hudson River. It was designed by I. M. Pei and Associates and completed in 1986. The structure was designed to accommodate huge conventions, but its presence has also helped greatly to improve the surrounding area of Clinton (Hell's Kitchen).

TOP: The Metropolitan Life Building's clock tower, along with the Flatiron Building, was a symbol of the business district of the early 1900s. Built in 1909, the *Met-Life* briefly held the record as the world's tallest building. It still has the world's largest clock face, with its 1,000-pound minute hands.

SHOPPING IN MANHATTAN

A. T. Stewart, the first true department store in the United States, opened its doors on lower Broadway in the mid-nineteenth century. By the 1880s the area on Sixth Avenue extending from 14th to 23rd streets was dubbed the Ladies' Shopping Mile, or Fashion Row, and the ornately decorated buildings that once housed such emporiums as Siegel-Cooper Dry Goods are still here.

You could spend a fortune in some of the stores along Madison, Fifth, and Park avenues. Or you might find extraordinary bargains and unique items in shops and boutiques all over New York. And the holiday decorations of the city's stores along Fifth Avenue make window shopping an event in itself.

The widest selection and the convenience of one-stop shopping are available at some of the major department stores. Macy's, which fills a city block (bordered by Sixth and Seventh avenues and West 34th and 35th streets), and Bloomingdale's (also known as Bloomie's), at 59th Street and Lexington Avenue, should be at the top of your list.

A visit to more-prestigious stores on Fifth and Madison avenues can begin at Saks Fifth Avenue, at 50th Street and Fifth Avenue. In the area of 57th Street and Fifth are Henri Bendel, Bergdorf Goodman, and the newer Galeries Lafayette, which all offer high fashion. Tiffany displays exquisite jewelry, Steuben presents carefully crafted crystal, and F. A. O. Schwarz provides an array of toys that delight young and old alike. During your shopping spree, be sure to stop off at Trump Tower at 57th Street and Fifth Avenue for lunch or tea among the marble-walled waterfalls. And Manhattan's most-exclusive stores can be found along Madison Avenue, above East 60th Street.

At the other end of the spectrum, you'll find a bazaarlike setting, where street vendors and small shops on Broadway from Astor Place down to Canal Street offer bargain prices and a grab-bag selection—from hats to hosiery, pots and pans to bedding, and art supplies to hardware. Shops in Greenwich Village and SoHo satisfy more-unusual tastes. Orchard Street on the Lower East Side is the place to look for discounted designer clothing.

Polly's restaurant in Greenwich Village was a favorite of artists, writers, and freethinkers in the World War I era, as shown in this 1920 photograph. In its cozy confines art, psychoanalysis, socialism, and free love were often passionately discussed over coffee and an inexpensive meal.

Union Square was once an arena for soapbox orators and political rallies, but now it's the site of New York's largest produce market every Wednesday, Friday, and Saturday.

WHEN LIFE IS VERY STRENUOUS AND SPIRITS ARE WAY DOWN
YOU'D BETTER GO TO POLLY'S IN LITTLE GREENWICH TOWN
FOR THERE THE CLANS ARE GATHERED - ITS THERE YOU'LL FIND EM ALL
THE ARTISTS AND THE WRITERS RANGED ALONG THE WALL.
MISS POLLY TAKES THE MONEY AND MIKE SAYS HE JUST CAN'T
WAIT ANY FASTER ON THE FOLKS IN POLLY'S RES-TAU-RANT
J.T.B.

GREENWICH VILLAGE - NEW YORK

JESSIE TARBOX BEALS

24

PART 3

MIDTOWN MANHATTAN

PAGE 26: This is the image in the mind's eye of midtown Manhattan: a concentration of massive, glittering structures topped by Art Deco spires, all filled with fast-moving business-people...throngs of office workers and shoppers buying a quick lunch from sidewalk vendors...the New York symphony of traffic and construction sounds.

PAGE 27: White lights illuminate the Empire State Building's upper thirty floors. The display is color-coordinated for the holidays and special events. Nighttime views from the 86th- and 102nd-floor observatories are truly spectacular. Both of the observatories are open until midnight every night.

Rockefeller Center is the location of Radio City Music Hall. The first Rockettes danced here in 1932, and today's troupe still does those famed synchronized high kicks. The lavish shows at the music hall are geared toward family entertainment. The complex is also the site of NBC's television studios where such programs as the "Today Show," "Donahue," "Saturday Night Live," and "Late Night with David Letterman" are produced.

The dramatic rise of the 850-foot RCA Building identifies Rockefeller Center, a complex of structures in the heart of midtown Manhattan, at the corner of West 50th Street and Avenue of the Americas (still called Sixth Avenue by long-term city residents). In winter, hurried holiday shoppers pause to watch carefree ice skaters gliding across the sunken outdoor plaza's frozen surface; during the warmer months sightseers and businesspeople relax under shaded tables. Across Fifth Avenue is the gothic grandeur of St. Patrick's Cathedral, the country's largest Catholic church.

Some of the significant buildings that have given New York its identifiable skyline are clustered in midtown, which spreads between 34th and 59th streets, river to river. Many of these buildings house the centers of media and commerce that influence the imaginations and purse strings of the world. This is where you really have to look up or, better yet, look down—from the 102nd-floor observatory in the Empire State Building.

Perhaps the best-known midtown structure, the 102-story Empire State Building, at Fifth Avenue and 34th Street, was completed in 1931, during the depths of the Great Depression. Other examples of skyscraper architecture abound in midtown, and such structures as the Seagram, AT&T, McGraw-Hill, GM, Citicorp, CBS, and Pan Am buildings have had their champions or critics. In contrast to all these high rises, the revered New York Public Library has sat squarely on an entire city block at 42nd Street and Fifth Avenue since 1911. The proud marble lions that guard the library's entrance are forever stone faced, but fanciful decorations soften their appearance at holiday time.

At Madison Square Garden (33rd Street and Seventh Avenue) you can become a temporary New Yorker by applauding the Knicks' winning basket or cheering a saving play by the Rangers' goalie as he neatly flicks away the hockey puck. Children are thrilled by the Ice Capades and circus performances here. And at the Westminster Kennel Club's annual show at the Garden, it's almost as much fun to watch the animals' owners and handlers as it is to see the dogs themselves.

More cosmopolitan than the neighborhoods to its south, midtown's attraction is that it contains New York's major retail and entertainment areas. Most hotels are located here, as are many department and specialty stores, restaurants, nightclubs, and theaters.

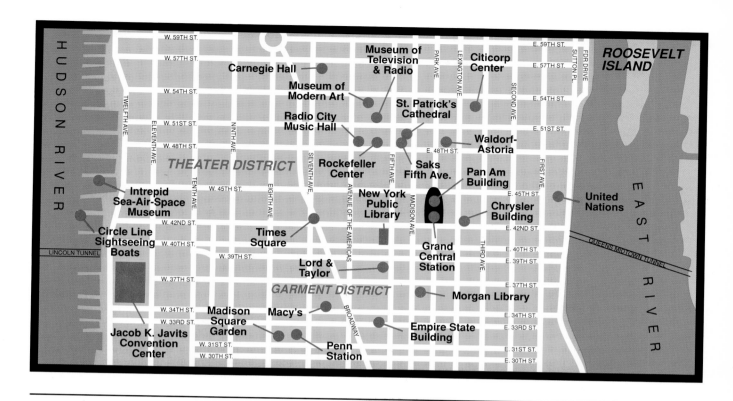

MIDTOWN MANHATTAN

Map not to scale. For a more complete listing of helpful area maps, please turn to page 64.

Saved by New York's Preservation Society, Grand Central Terminal is actually beneath the Pan Am Building, at 42nd Street and Park Avenue. The Beaux Arts-style station was constructed when the railroads were placed underground toward the end of the nineteenth century. A visit to Grand Central will momentarily take you back to a time when journeying by train offered the height in luxurious modern travel. Be sure to look up at the ceiling while you're there.

The gold-leaf statue of Prometheus, intended to glorify the individual, has presided over ice skaters in winter and outdoor diners in warm months since the 1930s. John D. Rockefeller's personal, yet all-American, motto on a plaque in the garden reads, "I believe in the supreme work of the individual and in his right to life, liberty, and the pursuit of happiness."

St. Patrick's Cathedral, between East 50th and 51st streets on Fifth Avenue, looks like a white-sugar wedding cake amid a forest of sleek office buildings. The cathedral was built in 1879 and is the largest Catholic church in the United States.

◀ Chicago may have been the birthplace of the skyscraper, but New York has turned it into an art form. The city's first skyscraper was put up at 50 Broadway but torn down after thirty years to make way for an even taller building. Seen here from the ground, Citicorp's asymmetrical modern wedge is illuminated under a full moon's glow.

BOTTOM: This aerial view of Manhattan's midtown, with the Empire State Building on the right, was taken in the mid-1930s, when New York was at its height as the modern American city.

◀ The Empire State Building may be everyone's idea of a perfect New York skyscraper. Although the World Trade Center's twin towers are taller, the Empire State Building continues to symbolize the glamour and essence of New York City and capture people's imaginations, as it has since 1931. The Guinness Book of Records Museum is housed here.

The Empire State Building was erected in the amazingly short period of two years in the early 1930s. New York writer E. B. White praised its construction: "It even managed to reach the highest point in the sky at the lowest point of the Depression. The Empire State Building shot twelve hundred and fifty feet into the air when it was madness to put out as much as six inches of new growth."

PERFORMING ARTS IN N.Y.C.

Dubbed the Great White Way for the blazing lights on its theater marquees, Broadway has been home to some of the best actors and writers and the most-applauded dramas, comedies, and musicals in the world.

Such American classics as *Our Town, Long Day's Journey into Night, Death of a Salesman,* and *Who's Afraid of Virginia Woolf?* have been produced here. Dramatic and musical performers have won a place in our hearts forever: John Barrymore, Helen Hayes, and Ethel Merman...Carol Channing, Sammy Davis, Jr., and Mary Martin, among scores of others.

The songs of Gershwin, Cole Porter, and Rodgers, Hart, and Hammerstein, still keep us humming today as we head to new musicals featuring compositions by Marvin Hamlisch or Stephen Sondheim. And the productions of such playwrights as Neil Simon and August Wilson bring us laughter and inspiration in the true tradition of Broadway theater.

Lincoln Center on the Upper West Side is the nerve center for dance and music in New York. In the complex are the New York Philharmonic—the oldest symphony orchestra in the United States—the American Philharmonic Orchestra, the New York State Theater, and the Juilliard School of Music. The Mostly Mozart Summer Music Festival is featured here, as are many performances by visiting orchestras.

The New York State Theater is the home of the New York City Ballet, directed by Peter Martins. Its School of American Ballet is one of the largest such dance schools in the country. The New York City Opera, which is also housed at the New York State Theater, is under the direction of Christopher Keene.

Across the way, the Metropolitan Opera House headlines some of opera's greatest stars: Jessye Norman, Placido Domingo, Luciano Pavarotti, and Kathleen Battle, among others. Formerly under the leadership of Mikhail Baryshnikov, the American Ballet Theater is located here, and the ABT also showcases many other major companies from around the world besides offering its own performances.

Another setting for everything from ballet to modern dance is the Moorish-style City Center Theater, between Sixth and Seventh avenues on West 55th Street. At various times here you can see the world-renowned performances of the Joffrey Ballet, the Alvin Ailey Company, and the Dance Theater of Harlem, as well as the works of two pacesetters of modern choreography—Paul Taylor and Merce Cunningham.

Beyond Manhattan the mainstay for New York dance enthusiasts is the Brooklyn Academy of Music. Three theaters occupy the main building—the Opera House, the Carey Playhouse, and the smaller Lepercq Space. The Ballet America series here is a national celebration of dance for visiting companies from all over the United States. The troupes of Martha Graham and José Limon have also been regular visitors.

A Carnegie Hall concert has always been a treat for lovers of such diverse performers as Benny Goodman, Rosemary Clooney, and Frank Sinatra, the Preservation Hall Jazz Band, Judy Collins, and PDQ Bach.

Not all the performing arts are found in formal surroundings. The city spills over with performances in colleges, libraries, churches, and parks, as well as in the cafés, clubs, and night spots that dot New York.

The lure of Broadway's bright lights attracts many young performers to the city to make their reputations in the theater. And New York has it all: musical comedy, serious drama, and avant-garde productions, whether in Broadway, off-Broadway, or off–off-Broadway theaters. A trip to New York would not be complete without seeing at least one performance.

Music, theater, and dance performances can be found in unexpected places all over New York City. Here, a dancer performs elegantly in the glass-enclosed Winter Garden of the World Financial Center, located in Battery Park City.

A uniquely American invention, musical theater reached the height of its popularity in New York City from the 1940s through the 1960s. Most musicals produced during that period were also later re-created on film in Hollywood: *Mame, Pal Joey, Oklahoma!, Carousel, South Pacific, The King and I, West Side Story,* and *Guys and Dolls* are just a few to come out of that period.

New York is full of luxury hotels, and one of the most admired is the Waldorf Astoria. Originally built by William Waldorf Astor on the site now occupied by the Empire State Building, today the hotel is located at Park Avenue and 50th Street. Its authentic Art Deco–style lobby, reminiscent of a gracious and sparkling era, makes a delightful meeting place.

RIGHT BOTTOM: Docked at Pier 86 at the Hudson River and West 46th Street, the *Intrepid* Sea-Air-Space Museum is uniquely housed in a U.S. naval aircraft carrier. The exhibits in the five main theme halls span the history and technology of sea, air, and space science from their beginnings through the twentieth century.

Times Square was once called
the crossroads of the world, and
it certainly appears that way
when it's crowded with throngs
of celebrants on New Year's Eve.
But on any day of the year you'll
find this famous landmark as
active and kaleidoscopic at
midnight as at midday.

The New York Public Library sits on an entire city block at Fifth Avenue and 42nd Street. The crouching white marble lions have been guarding the entrance since construction was finished in 1911. The library's layout is the result of a unique collaboration between librarians and architects. Books are not loaned out, but everyone is welcome to read from the twenty million books and documents inside the library. Scholars, famous and yet-to-be-famous writers, researchers, and average citizens use its resources on a daily basis.

A mosaic in the Art Deco style depicts industry and commerce. This is another of John D. Rockefeller's favorite themes evident in the major art works throughout the Rockefeller Center complex.

PART 4

UPPER EAST & WEST SIDES, CENTRAL PARK & NORTHERN MANHATTAN

PAGE 40: Hansom cabs—reminders of another century—wait for fares on Central Park South in front of the Plaza Hotel. The slower pace of the stately cabs allows sightseers and New Yorkers alike to capture the romance of the park.

PAGE 41: The minutely detailed bronze statue of Alice in Wonderland sitting on a mushroom attracts children like a magnet. It is located at the northern end of the Model Boat Basin just off East 75th Street. In addition to Alice, there are other statues depicting the March Hare and the Dormouse from Alice's famous tea party. All the statues are faithful to the original illustrations in Lewis Carroll's 1865 book.

Carnegie Hall, long a symbol of artistic success, was almost torn down in the 1960s. The vigorous efforts of many artists, led by violinist Isaac Stern, prevented its destruction. Even a short list of musical artists who have performed on its stage reads like a *Who's Who* of music: Tchaikovsky, Paderewski, Saint-Saëns, Rubinstein, Stravinsky, and Rachmaninoff.

Elegant and spacious apartment buildings were constructed along Riverside Drive and Central Park West in the mid-nineteenth century to coincide with the completion of Central Park. The Dakota, at Central Park West and 72nd Street, is an example of such a stylish apartment house. Nearby are the American Museum of Natural History and the Hayden Planetarium, at Central Park West and 79th Street.

By the late 1950s this portion of the Upper West Side had greatly declined. Since the construction of the Lincoln Center for the Performing Arts in the mid-1960s, however, the Upper West Side has undergone a gradual renewal. It is now a progressive, integrated area where actors, artists, writers, and musicians live alongside families and white-and blue-collar workers in thriving neighborhood communities. The area is now the site of restaurants, boutiques, book shops, and ethnically diverse greenmarkets and delicatessens.

At Amsterdam and 112th Street is an unusual building: the Cathedral Church of St. John the Divine, begun in 1892, is still being constructed a century later. When complete, this Episcopal cathedral will be one of the largest structures of its kind in the world.

The Upper East Side is the refuge of old and new money. Many of New York's museums, art galleries, antique shops, and consulates are clustered around Fifth and Madison avenues between East 59th and 96th streets.

Along the portion of Fifth Avenue once called Millionaires' Row, now known as the Museum Mile (79th to 104th streets), are the nineteenth-century mansions that the Astors, Vanderbilts, Whitneys, and Carnegies once called home. Many of these now shelter priceless art collections, as well as private schools and foreign diplomats. The greatest concentration of museums is between 70th and 90th streets, with the Frick at the southern end, and the Cooper-Hewitt at the northern.

In northern Manhattan, Harlem and Washington Heights (nicknamed Quisqueya Heights for its large Dominican population), on the west, and East Harlem (called El Barrio, and once known as Spanish Harlem), begin at the northern borders of Central Park.

Harlem's lively main thoroughfare is West 125th Street. There are many interesting landmarks to see in the region: Strivers Row, a collection of row houses designed at the turn of the century by Stanford White, New York's distinguished architect; the Apollo Theater; the Abyssinian Baptist Church (the oldest black church in the city); the Schomburg Center for Research in Black Culture; and the Morris-Jumel Mansion and the Hamilton Grange, which date from the eighteenth century.

On either side of Fifth Avenue are Washington Heights on the west, stretching north from 130th Street, and El Barrio on the east, north of 96th Street. These neighborhoods are home to a large and lively population of Puerto Ricans and Dominicans, as well as Cubans, West Indians, and Mexicans. La Marqueta, which runs up Park Avenue between East 111th and 116th streets, is a colorful outdoor market in El Barrio.

Near the northwestern tip of Manhattan, past the George Washington Bridge, is the Cloisters. Overlooking the Hudson River, this branch of the Metropolitan Museum of Art was opened in 1938. Exhibits here are limited exclusively to art of the Middle Ages, and you will step far back in time as you explore the four medieval cloisters, chapel, arcade, and fragrant herbal gardens.

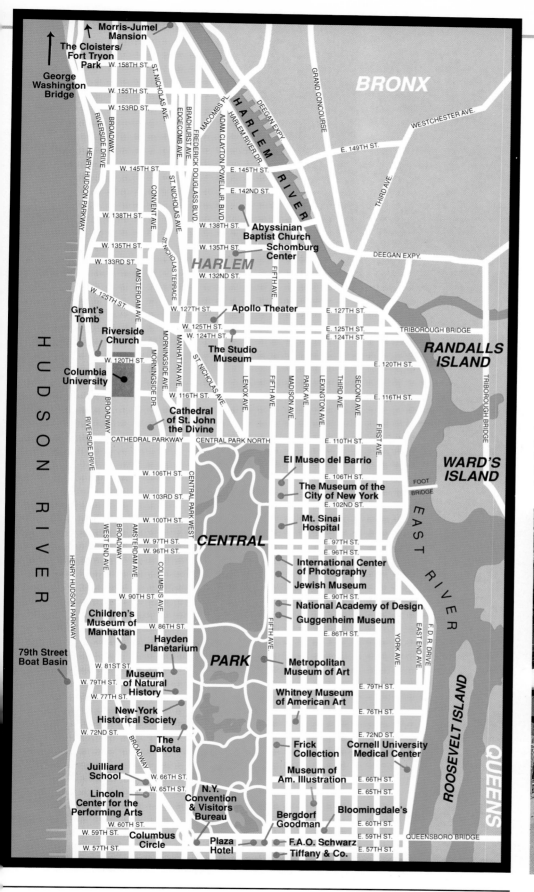

→ Morris-Jumel Mansion

↑ The Cloisters/ Fort Tryon Park

George Washington Bridge

W. 158TH ST.
W. 155TH ST.
W. 153RD ST.
W. 145TH ST.
W. 138TH ST.
W. 135TH ST.
W. 133RD ST.
W. 125TH ST.
W. 127TH ST.
W. 125TH ST.
W. 124TH ST.
W. 120TH ST.
W. 116TH ST.
W. 106TH ST.
W. 103RD ST.
W. 100TH ST.
W. 97TH ST.
W. 96TH ST.
W. 90TH ST.
W. 86TH ST.
W. 81ST ST.
W. 79TH ST.
W. 77TH ST.
W. 72ND ST.
W. 66TH ST.
W. 65TH ST.
W. 60TH ST.
W. 59TH ST.
W. 57TH ST.

BRONX

GRAND CONCOURSE

WESTCHESTER AVE.

E. 149TH ST.

E. 145TH ST.
E. 142ND ST.

DEEGAN EXPY.

HARLEM RIVER

HARLEM

Abyssinian Baptist Church
Schomburg Center

Grant's Tomb

Riverside Church

Columbia University

Apollo Theater

The Studio Museum

Cathedral of St. John the Divine

RANDALLS ISLAND

TRIBOROUGH BRIDGE

E. 127TH ST.
E. 125TH ST.
E. 124TH ST.
E. 120TH ST.
E. 116TH ST.
E. 110TH ST.
E. 106TH ST.
E. 102ND ST.
E. 97TH ST.
E. 96TH ST.
E. 90TH ST.
E. 86TH ST.
E. 79TH ST.
E. 76TH ST.
E. 72ND ST.
E. 66TH ST.
E. 65TH ST.
E. 60TH ST.
E. 59TH ST.
E. 57TH ST.

CATHEDRAL PARKWAY
CENTRAL PARK NORTH

El Museo del Barrio

The Museum of the City of New York

Mt. Sinai Hospital

WARD'S ISLAND

FOOT BRIDGE

International Center of Photography

Jewish Museum

National Academy of Design

Guggenheim Museum

CENTRAL

PARK

Children's Museum of Manhattan

Hayden Planetarium

79th Street Boat Basin

Museum of Natural History

New-York Historical Society

The Dakota

Juilliard School

Lincoln Center for the Performing Arts

Columbus Circle

Metropolitan Museum of Art

Whitney Museum of American Art

Frick Collection

Cornell University Medical Center

Museum of Am. Illustration

N.Y. Convention & Visitors Bureau

Bergdorf Goodman

Bloomingdale's

Plaza Hotel

F.A.O. Schwarz

Tiffany & Co.

EAST RIVER

ROOSEVELT ISLAND

QUEENS

QUEENSBORO BRIDGE

HUDSON RIVER

HENRY HUDSON PARKWAY
RIVERSIDE DRIVE
BROADWAY
RIVERSIDE DRIVE
ST. NICHOLAS AVE.
EDGECOMB AVE.
BRADHURST AVE.
FREDERICK DOUGLASS BLVD.
ADAM CLAYTON POWELL JR. BLVD.
MACOMBS PL.
HARLEM RIVER DR.
DEEGAN EXPY.
CONVENT AVE.
AMSTERDAM AVE.
ST. NICHOLAS TERRACE
MORNINGSIDE AVE.
MORNINGSIDE DR.
MANHATTAN AVE.
ST. NICHOLAS AVE.
LENOX AVE.
FIFTH AVE.
MADISON AVE.
PARK AVE.
LEXINGTON AVE.
THIRD AVE.
SECOND AVE.
FIRST AVE.
THIRD AVE.
DEEGAN EXPY.
TRIBOROUGH BRIDGE
F.D.R. DRIVE
EAST END AVE.
YORK AVE.
FIFTH AVE.
CENTRAL PARK WEST
BROADWAY
WEST END AVE.
AMSTERDAM AVE.
COLUMBUS AVE.
BROADWAY

When the weather is fine and warm in New York City, cafés, such as this one on Columbus Avenue on the Upper West Side, break out the tables and chairs for sidewalk dining, creating some of the best areas for people watching in the city.

▼

MUSIC

UPPER EAST & WEST SIDES
CENTRAL PARK & NORTHERN MANHATTAN

Map not to scale. For a more complete listing of helpful area maps, please turn to page 64.

CENTRAL PARK

New York had grown so quickly by the 1850s that land for picnicking and strolling seemed nonexistent, so resourceful New Yorkers took their sweethearts and families to the green, open spaces of the cemeteries in the outer boroughs of Queens and Brooklyn. William Cullen Bryant, the co-owner and editor of the New York *Evening Post*, loudly condemned this situation, with the result that eighty acres were purchased north of the city for public parkland.

How Central Park grew from 80 to 840 acres was the result of the less-than-generous aims of William Marcy ("Boss") Tweed. He convinced the city to purchase additional, swampy land that he and his friends just happened to own—at $7,500 an acre.

Fortunately for New York and all who visit today, world-renowned landscape architect Frederick Law Olmsted and his assistant Calvert Vaux won the contest for the best design of Central Park. They were able to transform what had been, according to Olmsted, "a pestilential spot, where rank vegetation and miasmatic odors taint every breath of air" into a park that would "lift the mind out of the moods and habits of city life."

Situated squarely between the upper west and east sides, the park is bordered by 59th Street (Central Park South), 110th Street (Central Park North), Fifth Avenue (to the east), and Central Park West. Central Park's design was unique for its time: gently rolling hills and grassy lawns, footpaths throughout the park, and underpasses. A carriage road circling the park was deliberately designed with twists and turns to discourage buggy racing, a popular diversion in the 1850s.

▲

During any given lunch hour, executives in business clothes can be seen alongside children playing in Central Park. In the boathouse near the pond is stored an entire fleet of model ships, brought out in June for an annual regatta.

A visit to the Central Park Zoo, located off Fifth Avenue at East 64th Street, is a delightful way to start a tour of the park. Although small, the recently renovated habitats are well maintained. Nearby is the children's zoo, where the gates are no taller than the average five-year-old child.

Most of the statuary in Central Park has been donated by New York philanthropists. There are many statues, such as this one of the German poet Friedrich von Schiller, that memorialize poets, writers, artists, and musicians, who contributed—directly or indirectly—to New York's culture.

PAGES 44 & 45: Surrounding Central Park on all sides, the Manhattan skyline provides sharp contrast to the green and lush tranquility of the park. Frederick Law Olmsted's brilliant design of the park resulted in accessibility and activities for all New Yorkers. The famous Shakespeare in the Park festival and New York Marathon attract thousands of visitors in the summer and fall, while horseback riding, jogging, roller-skating, and visiting the zoos are popular year-round activities.

HIGHLIGHTS

1. LASKER RINK & POOL
2. CLEOPATRA'S NEEDLE (Obelisk)
3. DELACORTE THEATER
4. BELVEDERE (The Castle)
5. SHAKESPEARE GARDEN
6. SWEDISH COTTAGE
7. BOW BRIDGE
8. LOEB BOATHOUSE
9. ALICE IN WONDERLAND
10. HANS CHRISTIAN ANDERSEN
11. CONSERVATORY WATER (Model Sailboat Pond)
12. BETHESDA FOUNTAIN & TERRACE
13. CHERRY HILL
14. STRAWBERRY FIELDS (John Lennon Memorial)
15. MINERAL SPRINGS PAVILION
16. TAVERN ON THE GREEN
17. LEHMAN CHILDREN'S ZOO
18. DAIRY (Visitor's Center)
19. CAROUSEL
20. CHESS & CHECKERS HOUSE
21. WOLLMAN RINK

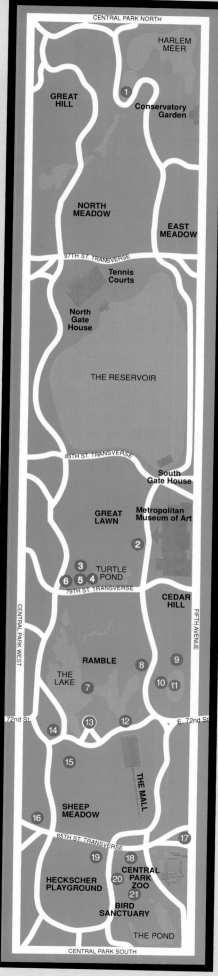

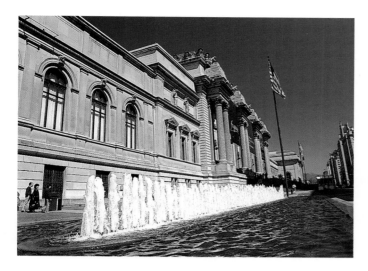

OPPOSITE: The Plaza Hotel is an unofficial landmark to many New Yorkers. Strauss is played in the gilt and white dining room, while the Oak Bar is a famed evening meeting place for friends.

▶ Plan to spend at least several days in the distinguished Metropolitan Museum of Art if you want to see everything displayed in the galleries that span four city blocks. Enter from Fifth Avenue to see the magnificent Tiffany windows. Works by El Greco, Rembrandt, Vermeer, and Goya are only a few of those in the enormous collection here.

▶ At one time a stroll along Fifth Avenue on Easter Sunday morning was a social necessity. Ladies showed off their finery while escorted by gentlemen in top hats, as in this 1905 photograph. This springtime tradition still continues, but nowadays an "Easter bonnet, with all the frills upon it," if worn at all, is consistent with today's fashion tastes.

Built in the mid-1960s, the Lincoln Center of the Performing Arts complex houses the New York Philharmonic, New York State Theater, Vivian Beaumont Theater, New York City Ballet, and Juilliard School of Music, as well as an annex of the New York Public Library that specializes in the performing arts. The grand Metropolitan Opera House's brightly colored paintings by Marc Chagall are visible in the picture shown here.

▲

Chorus girls line up in 1920 in one of Harlem's many clubs, which included Bamille, Connor's, Mexico's, Tillie's Inn, Ed Small's Paradise, Connie's Inn, and the gaudiest of them all, the Cotton Club. These dancers' unique costumes hint that their act displayed a popular jungle motif.

◄

Although the 1920s saw many talented musicians, Duke Ellington can be singled out for his contribution to jazz and the longevity of a career that spanned more than fifty years. Ellington and his orchestra opened at the Cotton Club in Harlem on December 4, 1927. His compositions include "Solitude," "Mood Indigo," "Satin Doll," "Black and Tan Fantasy," "Take the A Train," and many more.

HARLEM'S HEYDAY

The idea of today's Harlem conjures up many images, most gathered from the media. But there was a time during the short-lived Harlem Renaissance—what African-American writer Langston Hughes called the "Negro vogue" of the 1920s—that the eyes of both black and white intellectuals were focused on Harlem's creative artists.

Harlem in the 1920s was *the* place to go for anyone interested in jazz, top entertainment, or simply to be seen. Uptown hot spots included the Cotton Club, Baby Grand's, Sutton's, Wilt Small's Paradise, and Connie's Inn. Patrons, mostly wealthy whites from downtown, went as tourists to hear exciting new music being performed by Duke Ellington, Josephine Baker, Cab Calloway, Count Basie, Louis Armstrong, Ethel Waters, Eubie Blake, and many more.

The irony was that, as more whites from downtown crowded into the Harlem nightspots, the clubs often became too expensive for the average Harlemite. And whether owned and operated by whites or blacks, many places allowed only white customers.

Perhaps it was because of these circumstances that the trend of the Harlem rent party began. These affairs were also called whist parties or dances. They offered not only a chance to earn one's rent, but also to enjoy an evening's entertainment and refreshments for less money, and probably more fun, than at a nightclub. An invitation of the time reads: *If sweet mamma is running wild, and you are looking for a do-right child, just come around and linger awhile at a social whist party given by Pinkney & Epps.*

That era of black creativity was not limited to entertainers; it also included a bevy of talented artists, writers, thinkers, and activists. Paul Robeson, for example, held a degree in law from Columbia University and was a gifted athlete, singer, and eloquent spokesman for blacks. Marcus Garvey was the respected leader of a strong "back to Africa" movement. Just a few of the writers who flourished during and after that pioneering era were Langston Hughes, Jean Toomer, W. E. B. Du Bois, Ralph Ellison, Rudolph Fisher, and Countee Cullen.

We build our temples for tomorrow, strong as we know how, and we stand on top of the mountain, free within ourselves.

—LANGSTON HUGHES

The fifteen-year period following World War I was a time of creativity, hope, high spirits, and prosperity for many blacks in Harlem during a period called the Harlem Renaissance. These fashionably dressed 1920s Harlem belles are strolling along Seventh Avenue.

Map not to scale. For a more complete listing of helpful area maps, please turn to page 64.

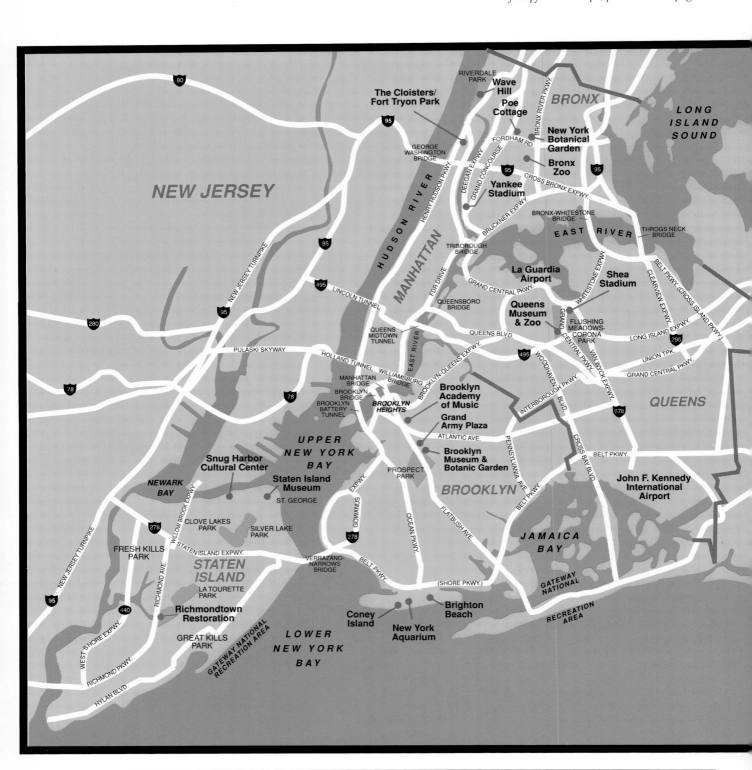

OUTER BOROUGHS

THE BRONX

PART 5

OUTER BOROUGHS

QUEENS

BROOKLYN

STATEN ISLAND

THE BRONX

PAGE 53: Founded in 1899 by the New York Zoological Society, the Bronx Zoo is the largest urban zoo in the nation. One of the newest exhibits is the Baboon Reserve, whose two-acre open landscape is one of the world's largest in a zoo. You can see nocturnal animals moving about in the World of Darkness, and birds soar freely in their three-story aviary in the World of Birds. The children's zoo combines education and fun with its participatory devices. Youngsters can crawl into a giant snail shell, investigate an enormous spider web, or curl up in a child-size bird's nest.

Home to the American League's Yankees, and able to seat up to 54,000 spectators, Yankee Stadium was built in 1923. It acheived near-mythological status over the years as such baseball greats as Babe Ruth, Lou Gehrig, Roger Maris, Mickey Mantle, and Joe DiMaggio thrilled the fans with their skill and their personalities.

Although it has changed over time, the name *The Bronx* comes from that of Jonas Bronck, a Danish farmer who, in 1639, settled five hundred wooded acres across the Harlem River from Manhattan.

A small tract of the original forest still thrives in the Bronx Park at the heart of the New York Botanical Garden, which includes the Enid A. Haupt Conservatory. Nearby is the acclaimed 265-acre Bronx Zoo. Its main gate, decorated with bronze animal figures, leads to the exhibits of the zoo's 675 animal species. A monorail will take you around the park above the animals that roam freely in their habitats. A world leader in conservation, the Bronx Zoo also pioneered the use of free-range landscapes with the opening of its African Plains exhibit in 1941.

In Riverdale a twenty-eight-acre enclave named Wave Hill overlooks the Hudson River. It has attracted such tenants as Theodore Roosevelt, Mark Twain, and Arturo Toscanini. Now a public arboretum, Wave Hill's manicured grounds contain sculpture and rare plants. Chamber music concerts are held here on Sunday afternoons.

Fordham University is in the Bronx, as is Yankee Stadium, home of the popular New York Yankees.

Located on Kingsbridge Road near the Grand Concourse in the Bronx, Poe Cottage is a small, white clapboard house that Edgar Allan Poe rented for $100 a year. Poe brought his ailing wife here in 1846, hoping in vain that the country air would do her some good. The author lived here for another two years after his wife died, until his own death in 1849. Poe wrote some of his finest works here: *The Bells, Ulalume, Eureka,* and *Annabel Lee.*

In the lush surroundings of the 250-acre New York Botanical Garden sits a gem of a building. Inspired by London's Crystal Palace, the Enid A. Haupt Conservatory is a shimmering glass structure that soars ninety feet above an elegant palm court. The conservatory also houses desert and tropical plants, a fern forest, and seasonal flower displays. Plan your visit to allow for a delightful lunch stop here.

QUEENS

Queens may be the first stop for many visitors to New York: both the La Guardia and John F. Kennedy airports are located here. And easy subway access to Manhattan helps to make Queens a desirable residential area.

Across the East River from Manhattan, this is a borough full of greenery. Planned communities integrate sports fields, parks, and community centers with landscaped residential areas. Like the rest of the city, Queens is a culturally diverse borough; Astoria, for example, has a large population of Greeks.

Isamu Noguchi, whose works contributed to the modern abstract art movement, maintained his studio in Queens. His work can be seen on Wednesdays and Saturdays from April through November at the Isamu Noguchi Garden Museum, located in the sculptor's former studio.

Queens was once the movie capital of the United States, and silent films and early talkies were produced here before the industry flourished in California. Today the Kaufman/Astoria Movie Studios still thrive, and such notable film makers as Woody Allen still produce movies there. This is the site of the Museum of the Moving Image, and visitors are welcome.

PAGE 53: Queens is the place for such sports as horse racing, tennis, and baseball. The National League's New York Mets play ball at Shea Stadium in Flushing, and the U.S. Open is held nearby at the USTA National Tennis Center. Other Queens sporting events include horse racing in Jamaica at Aqueduct and professional and amateur tennis championship matches at the West Side Tennis Club in Forest Hills.

◀ Evidence of both the 1939 and 1964 world fairs can still be seen at Flushing Meadows Park in Queens. The great steel Unisphere from the 1964 fair dominates the area. Exhibitions still in use include the Queens Museum (formerly the 1964 New York City Pavilion), which features a New York diorama—a large-scale, accurate model of New York City. Also of interest here are the Theater in the Park, the World's Fair Marina, and the Hall of Science, with its hands-on displays for children.

Built in 1910, the Queensboro (59th Street) Bridge and the Long Island Railroad/Penn Station complex helped the formerly isolated borough of Queens to grow quickly over the following three decades. The bridge runs parallel to the aerial tramway that connects Roosevelt Island with Manhattan. ▶

Many of the communities of brownstone residences built in Queens during the nineteenth and early twentieth centuries were carefully planned to integrate gardens and greenbelts around private homes and apartment buildings. This concept of "garden-city planning" offered residents a retreat from the congestion of urban industrial life.

The giant weeping beech tree that shades the Kingsland House in Queens is the oldest living monument in New York City. It was planted in 1847 by Samuel Parsons, a nurseryman who brought the shoot from Belgium. It is said that all other weeping beeches in this country come from this one.

BROOKLYN

The most-populous of the boroughs, Brooklyn covers seventy square miles of Long Island's southwestern tip and boasts many attractions.

The Brooklyn Botanic Garden, Steinhardt Conservatory, and the Brooklyn Museum, whose substantial collection of Egyptian art rivals those in London and Cairo, are known far beyond New York. Sarah Bernhardt, Edwin Booth, Pavlova, and Enrico Caruso have all performed at the Brooklyn Academy of Music, one of the nations' oldest performing arts centers. Another of the borough's outstanding features is the 526-acre Prospect Park, which designers Olmsted and Vaux considered their masterpiece.

You'll find one of the world's largest collections of Victorian brownstone homes in Brooklyn Heights. At various times this area has been home to writers Walt Whitman, Hart Crane, Thomas Wolfe, Arthur Miller, and Norman Mailer.

A children's natural history museum, the New York Aquarium, Coney Island, and the Gateway National Recreation Area are just a few more of Brooklyn's highlights.

◀ The Brooklyn Botanic Garden has probably the most-beautiful Japanese gardens in the Western Hemisphere. One is the pond-and-hill garden designed by Takeo Shiota in 1913. It is full of symbolism; for example, the pond is shaped like the Japanese character for the word *heart*. The second garden, created in 1963, contains an exact replica of the fifteenth-century Buddhist temple of Kyoto. The abstract layout of the garden was designed for contemplation.

◀ Looking like a manicured English estate, the Brooklyn Botanic Garden is located behind the Brooklyn Museum. Among its unusual features are the Shakespeare Garden, the Fragrance Garden for the blind, and the Steinhardt Conservatory, which maintains tropical and desert plants. One of the largest rose gardens in the United States grows here. The cherry trees' pink blossoms are spectacular from late April to early May.

PAGE 53: Most of New York City's boroughs feature brownstone buildings, but Brooklyn is unique for its Greek Revival– and Federal-period brownstones, which have been carefully preserved. Brooklyn Heights is the center of the gentrified "Brownstone Belt." So many brownstone-faced houses went up all over New York during the mid-1800s, in fact, that New Yorkers habitually call any row house a brownstone—whatever the materials used in its construction.

Coney Island's popularity was at its height from the 1930s through the 1950s. As shown in this 1930s picture, thousands of New Yorkers at a time would flee to this Brooklyn beach to avoid the city's heat and enjoy a day at the amusement park.

Designed by John Roebling, a German immigrant, and engineered by his son Washington, the Brooklyn Bridge was completed in 1883. Construction was almost abandoned after John Roebling died and Washington was severly injured. In fact, the bridge might never have been finished had not Washington's wife Emily taken over supervision of the project.

STATEN ISLAND

PAGE 53: Ferries travel every half hour between St. George terminal on Staten Island and Battery Park ferry terminal in Manhattan. The Staten Island Ferry is a necessary form of transportation for the island's inhabitants, but it can also provide an inexpensive sight-seeing tour at only fifty cents for a round-trip ride.

Staten Island has long had a reputation as a tightly knit community, and many of its families date back to the early eighteenth century. The island's first residents, the Unami Indians, didn't want to leave, though—the Dutch had to buy the island on five different occasions from the warring tribe before they could call it their own. This view of Richmondtown is a lithograph from 1850.

▼

Once a playground of the wealthy, Staten Island (sometimes called by its old name of Richmond) is made up of rolling hills and gentle valleys. Located south of Manhattan, the island is accessible from Battery Park, at the southern tip of Manhattan, by a fifteen-minute ride on the Staten Island Ferry. The Verrazano Narrows Bridge connects the island to Brooklyn.

Sights to see in the St. George area include the Staten Island Museum, Children's Museum, and zoo. The Snug Harbor Cultural Center is an eighty-three-acre arts center that was once a home for retired sailors. At the Richmondtown restoration in the center of the island, daily life of the seventeenth, eighteenth, and nineteenth centuries is re-created. The nation's oldest standing little red schoolhouse, known as Voorlezers House, and the Staten Island Historic Museum can be seen here.

On Lighthouse Hill is a hidden treasure: one of the world's largest private collections of Tibetan art, at the Jacques Marchais Center of Tibetan Art.

St. George has been Staten Island's departure and landing area since Cornelius ("Commodore") Vanderbilt began making ferry runs between Staten Island and Manhattan in 1817. Today the boat passes by the Statue of Liberty, Governors Island, Ellis Island, and other engaging sights during its fifteen-minute run. Shown here is a historic view of the ferry terminal's interior.

The Richmondtown restoration on Staten Island is a living-history project depicting daily life in Cocclestown village over the last three centuries. Shown here is Bennett House. The Staten Island Historical Society is in the middle of the settlement. Another noteworthy restoration project, at the northern end of the island, is the Snug Harbor Cultural Center, which has become a hub for performing and visual artists from around the world.

Info

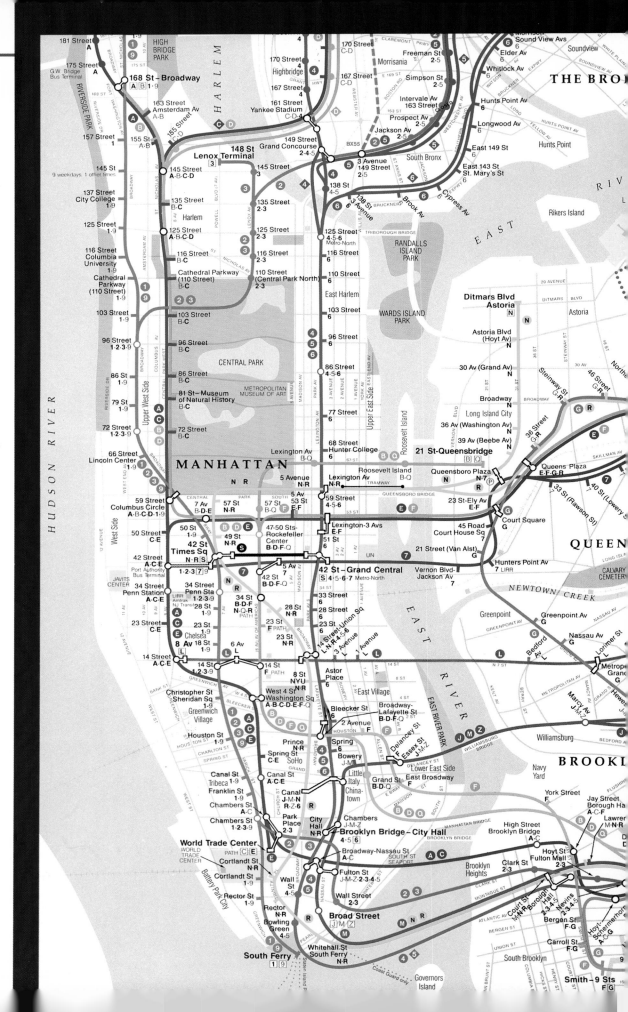

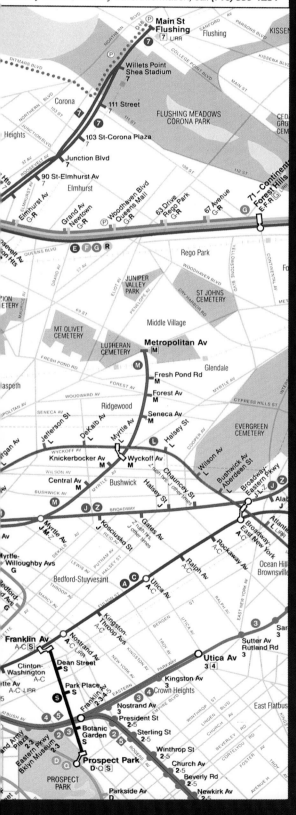

© New York City Transit Authority

GETTING AROUND

- Avenues run north to south; streets run east to west.

- Avenues increase in number from east to west; streets increase in number from south to north.

- Fifth Avenue is the dividing line between east and west Manhattan.

SUBWAYS

Subways remain the fastest way to get around New York City. For a $1.25 token you can travel as long or as short a distance as you would like. Study a map before going on the subway, however. These are available at any token booth or at the New York Convention and Visitors Bureau located at 2 Columbus Circle. The *Yellow Pages* also features subway maps for each borough.

As in most large cities, do not wear expensive jewelry or watches in public. It is also best to ride the subway between 7 a.m. and 7 p.m.

The New York subway system was built by immigrant laborers, mainly from Ireland. Taken in 1919, this photograph shows the construction of a tunnel for the 101st Street IRT station. New York subways still provide inexpensive and efficient transportation for commuters.

▼

SUGGESTED MAPS

- American Map, *Atlas of New York City, 5 Boroughs*
- Rand McNally, *Map of New York City*
- AAA, *New York Neighborhood Maps*
- Fodor's flashmaps, *Guide to New York*

USEFUL PHONE NUMBERS

- New York Convention and Visitors Bureau: (212) 397-8222
- Bus and subway Information: NYC Transit Authority: (718) 330-1234
- Time: (212) 976-1616
- Weather: (212) 976-1212
- Emergency: 911
- Immediate medical care: (212) 788-2830
- Information for the disabled: (212) 566-3913
- Sports information: (212) 976-1313
- Sightseeing services:
  - BACKSTAGE ON BROADWAY: (212) 575-8065
  - CIRCLE LINE TOURS: (212) 563-3200
  - GRAY LINE TOURS OF NEW YORK: (212) 397-2600
  - ISLAND HELICOPTER: (212) 683-4575
  - NBC STUDIOS TOUR: (212) 664-4444
  - NEW YORK STOCK EXCHANGE: (212) 656-5168
  - STATEN ISLAND FERRY: (212) 806-6941
  - UNITED NATIONS: (212) 963-7713

◀ Horse-drawn carriages, also known as hansom cabs, can be found all along 59th street (Central Park South) and Columbus Circle. This equine worker appears to be sharing its lunch with some friends.

Rockefeller Center takes on a fairy-tale quality during Christmas. The square is filled with twinkling lights and golden angels, and watching the lighting of the seven-story Christmas tree in the plaza is as much a national event as a local one. The outdoor dining area in the sunken plaza beneath the statue of Prometheus is turned into an ice-skating rink during winter months. ▶

BACK COVER: Most people must be content with watching Macy's Thanksgiving Day parade on television, but New Yorkers are lucky enough to be able to see this extraordinary annual spectacle for themselves.